100 Small Poems

———————

Nicholas Cairns

100 Small Poems

Contents

All of me... 6

Peacocks... 7

Him... 8

Bite... 9

Bi.. 10

Sorrow.. 11

Lifetime.. 12

Memories... 13

Ten.. 14

Ache.. 15

The Destination... 16

Empires.. 17

Living... 18

Dukebox... 19

Broken.. 20

The Wind... 21

Crack.. 22

Art/Word.. 23

World.. 24

Wave... 25

Skin and Bone... 26

Afterglow... 27

Warning... 28

Wingbeat.. 29

Change..30

Cage..31

Perfect...32

Mess...33

Frame by Frame..34

Some Day..35

Moonlight..36

Porcelain..37

Revenge..38

Revolution..39

Coming Out..40

Blink..41

Core...42

Bury Me...43

Watercolour..44

Stardust..45

Tomorrow...46

Persephone...47

Brand...48

Horizon..49

Bone..50

Wrecked...51

The Water..52

Choke..53

Flowers..54

Gone..55

100 Small Poems

Small House..56

Hunger..57

Limitless..58

The Writer..59

The Sky...60

This Night..61

Fine China..62

Roots..63

Snake..64

Heights..65

The Sun...66

Songs..67

Premonition..68

Haiku #1..69

Tired...70

The Climbing Tree..71

Haiku #2..72

Happiness..73

Leave..74

Ebb & Flow..75

The Rain..76

I Used to be in Love...77

Clean..78

The Beach..79

Icarus...80

Bed..81

Autumn..82

Tide...83

Garden..84

Island..85

Ending..86

Adrift..87

Kiss...88

Hollow..89

Egg..90

Broke..91

Sunrise (acrostic)..92

Endure..93

Journeys...94

Lockdown..95

Haiku #3..96

The Lake..97

Bluebells..98

Cruelty...99

Mountain..100

Something New..101

True Love...102

Snake-Eyes...103

Treasure..104

Gone...105

You tell me you'll love all of me

but believe me, you won't.

Inside every person you know

is a person you don't.

All of Me

Nicholas Cairns

Male peacocks have evolved

over years

to attract a mate,

feathers so elaborate

they can hardly fly.

To find love,

they gave up the sky.

Peacocks

Love lost is darkness, silence,

and so I light a candle and speak:

a song, a prayer, a hymn.

Him.

Him

Nicholas Cairns

The sting of you lingers

like the moon after night.

Who would've thought a kiss

could carry such a bite?

Bite

Eyes on the prize:

a chiselled jaw, a soft thigh,

a ruby lip, a meaty bi

cep.

That's the word.

polar lingual cycle sexual ology.

te me. Harder.

Bi

Nicholas Cairns

I've seen true sorrow,

it hides in plain sight,

with a smile and a sigh

and a *well, never mind.*

Sorrow

I could have you for a lifetime –

endless days with you near me.

I could hear your tales a thousand times

and never grow weary.

Lifetime

Nicholas Cairns

The memories hurt, so I try to replace

the sound of your laugh, that look on your face.

Memories

When I was ten years old

I found a dead bird by the road.

Now some of those I love the most

are corpses.

Ten

Nicholas Cairns

This sadness holds no tears,

just a heavy weight, a constant ache

for long gone golden years.

Ache

Nothing here is what you suppose.

I'm belladonna dressed as a rose.

The sweetest dove flanked by crows.

The sunlit path you almost chose

until you saw the destination

and froze.

The Destination

Nicholas Cairns

In the city of Rome

I walk streets steeped in worship

that has outlived the sun.

Prophecy and passion,

godly myths and great loves,

desire and dedication

immortalised

in marble, stone and rust,

and I think:

we have something in common,

the empires and us.

Empires

You live in words, I live in rhyme.

What you call living I call killing time.

Living

Nicholas Cairns

On the bar's dukebox,

the first song I ever knew.

It's happy and sad all at once.

It reminds me of you.

Dukebox

I love you

to the depths of me

I'm like you

in the best of me

I'll miss you

with the final, shaking, broken

breath of me.

Broken

Nicholas Cairns

I speak my grief into the breeze

in hopes the wind will set it free

and carry it on falling leaves

scattering amongst the trees

parting me from my misery

and leaving only memories.

The Wind

If we were made of water

we could swim around this wall.

If we were made of air

we could rise fifty feet tall,

but you and I are human –

heavy, flawed and whole,

and so the crash we face

is unavoidable.

Crash

Nicholas Cairns

Stroke me lightly with a brush

then hit me where it hurts.

I'm a true work of art.

I'm a real piece of work.

Art/Work

In the end, what can I say?

I love you,

even from a world away.

World

Nicholas Cairns

I'd love to live inside a wave,

watch it curve and dance above me,

and make a fleeting place that's safe

where nobody can touch me.

Wave

Did you take me with you?

Am I empty too?

I fear I'm nought but skin and bone,

and where my heart once was – a stone.

Skin and Bone

Nicholas Cairns

Somewhere in the afterglow

there's a place only lovers go.

I've meandered my way there before

but was turned away at the door.

Afterglow

A word of warning: that boy ain't right.

He'd dance with the devil to see you tonight.

Warning

Nicholas Cairns

They say the slightest shift can change the course of history –

a butterfly's wingbeat can send a nation reeling –

and I can't help but wonder,

if I could go back,

was there a time I could have saved you

with just a wave of my hand?

Wingbeat

You touched my leg and told me

that everything would change.

I didn't know that meant you too.

Change

You are everywhere:

a forcefield, a ghost.

How do I move on

when you are all I know?

Don't you see?

There is no better day.

I am the bird.

You are the cage.

Cage

I never claimed to be perfect.

Some things about me are remiss:

I drink too much and I get wrecked;

I greet strangers with a kiss;

I destroy things I should protect;

I fall for things I should dismiss.

Yes, I know I'm not perfect,

but fuck I don't deserve this.

Perfect

Nicholas Cairns

We've been to town,

we've messed around.

Your dress is stained,

my shoes are scuffed,

so why don't we just take them off?

Mess

A night to remember

frame by frame.

We went out together

and came home changed.

Frame by Frame

Nicholas Cairns

I still think of you, you know.

My silly heart thought things would last.

I still wait for you, in vain,

as summers end and seasons pass.

Despite time

and change

and loss

and space

I'll keep waiting.

Some day. Some place.

Some Day

I often wander alone at night

in hopes the delicate moonlight

might fix me,

illuminate my paper skin

and make me whole again.

Moonlight

Nicholas Cairns

I used to be made of metal,

stainless steel with iron eyes,

a gaze impenetrable

because iron eyes don't cry

but now my skin is thinner

and every touch leaves a crack.

You drop me and I shatter –

a delicate porcelain wreck.

Porcelain

I do revenge the long way,

you'll think you've won 'til one day,

when everything seems peaceful,

the truth ignites, you scramble,

reality falls into place

and you see that you've been played.

Revenge

Nicholas Cairns

The foundations are shaking

in this tired institution.

There's a word on the wind

and that word is

revolution.

Revolution

I leapt

out of hiding

and into hope,

like a cliff edge

in barren plains

descending

to the rich

blue

sea.

Coming Out

Nicholas Cairns

In the blink of an eye it came undone,

a broken breath on the rising sun.

Blink

The shades of my heart

are all faded grey-blues

save a core of deep red

with the outline of you.

Core

Nicholas Cairns

Don't bury me six feet under

and be surprised when I grow.

Bury Me

Colours bleeding, lines blurring,

sky and earth: a single stain.

Life is a watercolour

left out in the rain.

Watercolour

Nicholas Cairns

I stopped believing in magic

when you stopped believing in us.

Don't sell me desert sand

and tell me it's stardust.

Stardust

If tomorrow starts without me,

love, don't be surprised.

I'm a very different person

in the sobering sunrise.

So if you wake up alone

don't take it as a slight.

Some romances last forever.

Others last one night.

Tomorrow

Nicholas Cairns

I take a breather from my fate

and let the breeze blow clean my mind

(the humdrum summer

the splinter of winter)

before the voice inside calls me back

to the Dark Below.

Persephone

Don't tell me what to do.

Don't tell me how to feel.

Football in the park

wearing six-inch heels.

Don't tell me how to sit.

Don't tell me where I stand.

I don't want to be a boy,

I want to be a brand.

Brand

Nicholas Cairns

You soared into my heart, dark and surprising,

the shadow of a bird on a golden horizon.

Horizon

You spit and split and snap the bone,

a hunk of flesh, a slab of heart,

you grip and tear me all apart

until I am truly gone.

And while your teeth are wet with blood,

you call this love.

Bone

Nicholas Cairns

Weak as I am,

wrecked as I am,

worthless as I am,

I still deserve more than you.

Wrecked

Raindrops in spring, roses in June,

sunlight in February:

the best things in life are temporary.

That's what I tell myself since you left

and yet,

are you really gone?

After all, a wave exists no more

once it crashes on the shore

but the water,

the water

lives on.

The Water

Nicholas Cairns

Every time I share another's kiss

I hope you taste it on your lips.

Every time I wrap my hands

around a lover's throat

I hope you choke.

Choke

The flowers that frame our bed have succumbed to rot.

Petals fall from roses and sweet forget-me-nots.

Flowers

Nicholas Cairns

How can life go on?

They mustn't know what's wrong.

So I take to the streets,

fall to my knees,

and cry out:

He is gone!

He is gone!

He is gone!

Gone

In a small house down by the sea

the ghosts of us live happily.

I cannot bear to enter in

and discover what might have been.

Small House

Nicholas Cairns

Cancel the dinner plans, no just desserts,
enough talking now, no time for words,
sweet poems and bitter truths left at the door,
our clothes flung on the bedroom floor.
This is a different kind of hunger.

Hunger

For the longest time, you shaped me

like water in a glass –

I was trapped.

It took a smash

to show me how *limitless*

I really am.

Limitless

Nicholas Cairns

I don't give up control easily.

I only possess faith in me,

but for you

I'd tear apart this tome.

Maybe you could be the writer

and I could be the poem?

The Writer

Palms rise to the sky.

Maybe I could clutch it

and pull down a piece for myself –

warm and soft and blue;

it's as close as I can get

to the feeling of you.

The Sky

Nicholas Cairns

If this is it,

if this is really it now,

give me a second to appreciate how

beautiful you look

in this light.

I'll imprint upon my memory

the tragedy

of this night.

This Night

You clutch me like fine china,

bubble-wrapped and strapped in,

but I don't need protecting.

The worst's already happened.

Fine China

Nicholas Cairns

I don't grow like flowers,

I grow like roots.

Silently I spread

until I'm in the very

foundations

of you.

Roots

I shed you like a second skin

so in the tales you weave

I am painted as the snake

and you are gentle Eve,

but in the end, it matters not

how you choose to grieve –

I was already victorious

when I took my leave.

Snake

Nicholas Cairns

Listening to the trees,

I hear whispers in the leaves;

echoes sound from the heights

I one day hope to reach.

Heights

Grief is not the moon,

it is the sun.

It burns

when you linger too long.

It splits and blisters and roasts.

It sets you aflame.

You can't look too close.

But it's beautiful, in its way.

It warms me,

the sound of your name.

The Sun

Nicholas Cairns

The songs that bring you back to me

are both a blessing and a curse.

The sweetness of their symphony

makes silence so much worse.

Songs

I had a vision of a river

running backwards through the woods.

The sunlight glistened on the water,

the birdsong calm as motherhood.

I wandered along the riverbank,

following around each bend,

but the premonition broke just as

I saw you waiting at its end.

Premonition

Nicholas Cairns

Beauty hides darkness.

A city burning to dust

looks just like the dawn.

Haiku #1

Don't call me a taxi –

I can't face sobriety.

You say that you're tired,

but I know you're just tired of me.

Tired

Nicholas Cairns

Come on,

you count to three.

I'll hide

by the climbing tree,

but please

don't look for me.

I'm right

where I want to be.

The Climbing Tree

I write misery,

leave tears in my poetry

to free them from me.

Haiku #2

Nicholas Cairns

I find myself free-floating,

trembling yet triumphant,

untethered and widespread.

I have stopped sacrificing my happiness,

And sacrificed us instead.

Happiness

If I was you

I'd leave me too.

Leave

Nicholas Cairns

Grief is never steady –

it ebbs and it flows.

That's why I think of you

when I look at the sea.

Ebb & Flow

I never minded the rain

until the moment you left.

Now I can't help but think

the sky itself is bereft

and all the world is mourning you too.

The Rain

Nicholas Cairns

I used to be in love with the moon,

the way she makes the water dance.

I used to lie awake at night

and lift up both my hands

to the sky,

until one night

in the dark pre-dawn,

I found myself lost

in the eye of the storm

and my lover was nowhere in sight.

She retreated to safety,

hidden from me,

and I weathered that storm alone.

I Used to be in Love

Your fingerprints mark me

like a shameful tattoo;

a tangible regret

which I cannot undo,

but I'll forgive the mistakes

that I made at sixteen

and I'll watch that child grow

as I love myself clean.

Clean

Nicholas Cairns

Let's take a walk on the beach,

watch the sea erase our steps,

and pretend we never existed at all.

The Beach

What can I say? Just goes to show

we hurt the ones we love the most.

I am the sun. You flew too close.

Icarus

Nicholas Cairns

Grief is a bed I cannot leave,
sheets soft with memories
of you.

Bed

The beauty of the dying things

is too painful to view;

there was nothing glorious and gold

about the loss of you.

Autumn

Nicholas Cairns

By now, it's been three years

but still I wait patiently.

The shore has its heart broken

every morning by the sea,

yet the tide always returns

so maybe you'll come back to me.

Tide

I think I broke my soul

making room for you.

Such healing takes time

but one day I'll bloom

into a garden of flowers

overgrown and wild

where the trees reach the clouds

and the woods stretch for miles.

Garden

Nicholas Cairns

I would cast a stone into the sea

for each bittersweet memory

and make a pile beneath the waves

until an island takes its shape

then I would have somewhere to rest

and free the howl inside my chest

Island

I never said goodbye.

I just turned and you were gone,

like a song ending abruptly

while I'm still singing along.

Ending

Nicholas Cairns

Cast me adrift in a sea

with a surface still as glass.

My hand ripples the world.

Below me, birds fly past

and I am free at last.

Adrift

You say last night you bit the bullet

and kissed me in a dream.

No wonder you woke up looking like

the cat who got the cream.

Kiss

Nicholas Cairns

Grief is a wound

that never heals –

a mouth,

closed some days,

open others,

as though it breathes

like you did

on that morning:

hollow and rattling.

Hollow

There is a legend that claims

that the Earth is an egg

and that one day

the beast inside will hatch.

Well, if there's any truth

to that old verse,

I hope it eats you first.

Egg

Nicholas Cairns

I wish your love was a lie I could buy,

but you bled me dry one too many times.

Now it costs me a fortune when you name is spoken

and I'm left empty, broke and heartbroken.

Broke

Stars were always your favourite;

untold stories spanning galaxies.

Night skies drew your eyes,

rounding us all up to see.

I still look at the stars, you know.

Sunrises, they can keep.

Everyone knows true glory glows when all the world sleeps.

Sunrise (acrostic)

Nicholas Cairns

I sit at home like a child on the floor,

dreading the sound of your keys in the door,

never dreaming that I could be worth more

than a life with you that I simply endure.

Endure

What use it is to talk of journeys?

We've known our end from the start.

We're a river running to the sea,

no – veins flowing to the heart.

To change the course of destiny

would be to tear ourselves apart.

Journeys

Nicholas Cairns

Another stint in the cosy clink.

Lonely thoughts are ten a penny.

I like to give as good as I get

but I'm just not getting any.

Lockdown

I lost you at dawn;

both of us bathed in a glow

that you never saw.

Haiku #3

Nicholas Cairns

Kiss me

like the moon kisses the lake –

soft and lingering,

illuminating every secret

beneath my surface.

The Lake

You are the gardener of excuses,

sweet bluebells the colour of bruises.

With love and care, you harvest lies

while I watch, barren, and feign surprise.

Bluebells

Nicholas Cairns

Inhale the wine, exhale the truth,
find what we buried, unearth it:
I fell in love with your cruelty
because I thought I deserved it.

Cruelty

You batter and wail.

I am still standing.

You are the wind.

I am the mountain.

Mountain

Nicholas Cairns

Coat the dawn in pink and blue.

Listen out for something new.

Quickly, you surpassed me

but slowly, I outgrew you.

Something New

They say true love is tales of old

but what we had was fierce and new.

They say true love is red and gold

but I've never been so black and blue.

True Love

Nicholas Cairns

You called my name

and I was home.

It's such a shame

I left alone,

but I'm to blame,

I should have known

love is a game

with snake-eyes thrown.

Snake-Eyes

I wonder what it's like to be you.

Sunken treasure, something silver

shimmering just below the surface,

glistening in the sun,

distorted by the water,

always lying just out of reach.

Treasure

Nicholas Cairns

You told me time heals everything but I know you were wrong.

You can't mend a broken heart when a piece of it is gone.

Gone

Printed in Great Britain
by Amazon